The Weapons of World War I: A History of the ~~~~~, ~~~~~, Artillery, Gas, and Planes Used during the Great War

By Charles River Editors

A Russian tank

About Charles River Editors

Charles River Editors provides superior editing and original writing services across the digital publishing industry, with the expertise to create digital content for publishers across a vast range of subject matter. In addition to providing original digital content for third party publishers, we also republish civilization's greatest literary works, bringing them to new generations of readers via ebooks.

Sign up here to receive updates about free books as we publish them, and visit Our Kindle Author Page to browse today's free promotions and our most recently published Kindle titles.

Introduction

A British machine gun and crew

The Weapons of World War I

"God would never be cruel enough to create a cyclone as terrible as that Argonne battle. Only man would ever think of doing an awful thing like that. It looked like 'the abomination of desolation' must look like. And all through the long night those big guns flashed and growled just like the lightning and the thunder when it storms in the mountains at home. And, oh my, we had to pass the wounded. And some of them were on stretchers going back to the dressing stations, and some of them were lying around, moaning and twitching. And the dead were all along the road. And it was wet and cold. And it all made me think of the Bible and the story of the Anti-Christ and Armageddon. And I'm telling you the little log cabin in Wolf Valley in old Tennessee seemed a long long way off." - Alvin C. York

World War I, also known in its time as the "Great War" or the "War to End all Wars", was an unprecedented holocaust in terms of its sheer scale. Fought by men who hailed from all corners of the globe, it saw millions of soldiers do battle in brutal assaults of attrition which dragged on for months with little to no respite. Tens of millions of artillery shells and untold hundreds of millions of rifle and machine gun bullets were fired in a conflict that demonstrated man's capacity to kill each other on a heretofore unprecedented scale, and as always, such a war brought about technological innovation at a rate that made the boom of the Industrial Revolution seem stagnant.

Since the industrial revolution, arms and materiel output had increased by orders of magnitude, as had the quality and uniformity of the products. Several developments had already taken place in the years building up to the conflict, stepping stones towards the vast escalation in military innovation which took place immediately prior to and during World War I. Chief among these was the invention of smokeless gunpowder, which took place concurrently among several powers between 1890 and 1905. This was a crucial development, as it eliminated the literal "fog of war" which in vast quantities obscured the battlefield entirely and on an individual level both gave away the position of marksmen and made it impossible for them to fire accurately unless they moved away from their own smoke-cloud. Further innovations included the adoption into service of the first belt-fed machine guns, predecessors of those which would wreak such slaughter in the trenches, and the development of cannon which did not roll backwards after each shot as 19th century pieces did, but remained fixed in place.

The arms race before the war and the attempt to break the deadlock of the Western and Eastern Fronts by any means possible changed the face of battle in ways that would have previously been deemed unthinkable. Before 1914, flying machines were objects of public curiosity; the first flights of any account on rotor aircraft had been made less than 5 years before and were considered to be the province of daredevils and lunatics. By 1918, all the great powers were fielding squadrons of fighting aircraft armed with machine-guns and bombs, to say nothing of light reconnaissance planes. Tanks, a common feature on the battlefield by 1918, had not previously existed outside of the realm of science fiction stories written by authors like H.G. Wells. Machine guns had gone from being heavy, cumbersome pieces with elaborate water-cooling systems to single-man-portable, magazine-fed affairs like the Chauchat, the Lewis Gun and the M1918 BAR. To these grim innovations were added flame throwers, hand grenades, zeppelins, observation balloons, poison gas, and other improvements or inventions that revolutionized the face of warfare.

These technological developments led to an imbalance. Before the introduction of the man-portable light machine gun (which took place in the second half of the war), not to mention tanks (which also joined the fight late in the game), defensive firepower vastly outweighed offensive capability. Massed batteries of artillery, emplaced heavy machine guns, barbed wire entanglements, and bewildering fortifications meant that ground could not be taken except at incredible costs in human lives. This led to the (somewhat unjustified) criticism famously leveled at the generals of World War I that their soldiers were "lions led by donkeys". Certainly, every army that fought in the Great War had its share of officers, at all levels of command, who were incompetent, unsuitable, foolish, or just plain stupid, but there were plenty of seasoned professionals who understood their job and did it well. The main problem facing commanders in the war was that there was such a bewildering array of new armaments, with such vast destructive potential, that previous military doctrines were virtually useless. Cavalry, which had been expected to play a major role both as reconnaissance and as "mounted infantry", operating in much the same way as airborne and mechanized troops would later to rapidly outflank enemy positions, quickly proved useless. Frontal infantry assaults were cut to shreds by enemy defensive fire, but there seemed to be no major alternative. Ground had to be taken, even if at great cost, and to do so, more destructive weapons were devised, tested and deployed.

As a result, World War I was the first truly industrial war, and it created a paradigm which reached its zenith with World War II and towards which virtually all equipment, innovation and training were dedicated throughout the Cold War and the remainder of the 20th century. To this day, modern warfare remains synonymous with tanks and mass infantry battles, although a confrontation of this nature has not occurred (except briefly during Operation Desert Storm) since World War II.

The Weapons of World War I analyzes the technological advancements in weaponry that produced the deadliest conflict in history up to that time. Along with pictures of important people, places, and events, you will learn about the weapons of World War I like never before, in no time at all.

The Weapons of World War I: A History of the Guns, Tanks, Artillery, Gas, and Planes Used during the Great War

About Charles River Editors

Introduction

   Chapter 1: Up Close and Personal

   Chapter 2: Rapid Fire

   Chapter 3: The Steel Rain

   Chapter 4: Unstoppable Juggernauts

   Chapter 5: Airplanes

   Chapter 6: Miscellaneous Weapons

   Chapter 7: Conclusion

   Bibliography

Chapter 1: Up Close and Personal

Anyone with even a passing knowledge of military affairs understands that while they often lacked the glamour of cavalry and the raw killing power of artillery, infantry was the backbone of every army. Artillery could deny ground, while cavalry and tanks could take it, but only the infantry could hold it, and likewise only the infantry could operate, to an extent, independent of its support arms. Accordingly, the standard-issue weapons carried by conventional infantry in World War I remained crucial for the main belligerents in World War I, including the British Empire, Germany, France, Austria, Russia, Italy, and the United States.

Throughout World War I, the rifle was the main weapon for the infantry (and cavalry) forces of all the main belligerents. Submachine guns and assault rifles were still decades away, and man-portable light machine guns only appeared in the latter part of the conflict. The bolt-action rifle, which was versatile, reliable and capable of high accuracy and sustained rates of fire in the right hands, proved to be devastating when massed formations of infantry were targeted by marksmen in the trenches. Some countries chose to manufacture two different versions: a long rifle for infantry and a short carbine for cavalry, artillery and support arms. Others, like the British and Americans, opted for a mid-length weapon which would satisfy the requirements of both.

The overwhelming majority of the hundreds of thousands of British, Commonwealth and Imperial troops fighting in World War I did so armed with the famous "Smelly", the standard British longarm from 1907 to after the end of the Second World War (Mk IV variant). Chambered in the powerful .303 cartridge, it was sturdy, reliable, accurate to 500 yards (with an effective range of 1500+), had conventional iron sights, and was capable of up to 30 shots (or 20 aimed ones) a minute in the hands of a skilled rifleman. The Lee-Enfield, although it possessed a magazine, was fed by two 5-round stripper clips (strips of metal which locked cartridges in place and were removed by pushing the rounds down into the open bolt receptacle), and it could take an extra round in the barrel once both clips were fed in, giving it a 10+1 capacity. Much loved by the troops, it still sees active service today, including among the Taliban of Afghanistan.

Short Magazine Lee-Enfield (SMLE) Mark III

Entering service with the French Army in 1887, the Lebel, although revolutionary at the time of its creation as the first main service rifle to fire smokeless powder cartridges, was already somewhat outdated by the start of World War I, having been in service for more than a quarter of a century. Chambered in the French 8mm Lebel cartridge, it was accurate up to 400 yards and possessed an effective range of approximately 4 times that number. It carried 8 rounds in a tubular magazine below the barrel, with a further two in the transporter and chamber, an arrangement similar to the Winchester lever-action rifle. This slowed reloading time considerably since each round had to be fed into the magazine tube individually. The Lebel, although powerful, suffered from several issues, not least the fact that if a soldier lost count of the bullets and attempted to frenetically ram more cartridges into the magazine than would fit, the firing pin of the cartridge ahead could be detonated by the nose of the one behind, leading to catastrophic weapon failure and injury. Poor sights and other issues meant the rifle was quickly abandoned by most French Army units after World War I.

Fusil Lebel Modele 1886 (Carbine Variant)

The Russians relied on the Mosin-Nagant M91 (and subsequent variants), one of the most successful rifles ever manufactured. 35 million units were produced from 1891, mostly in Russia, although a million units were produced for the Russian Empire by American arms companies, and they were manufactured through the end of World War II. Chambered in the 7.62x54mmR cartridge (the father of the 7.62x39 round still in current service with many armed forces today), the Mosin-Nagant was accurate up to 400 yards (800+ with optics). It had a capacity of 5 rounds plus one in the chamber, and while it was configured to load stripper clips, shortages meant that troops often had to feed in the rounds individually, a less desirable solution. Its bolt action was smooth but heavy, reducing the number of aimed shots to around 10 a minute (taking into account the delay afforded by loading the weapon's rounds one by one).

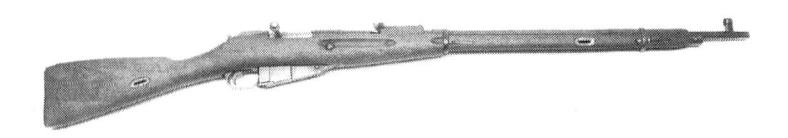

Mosin-Nagant M1891

Russian soldiers carrying the rifles during World War I

Italy's main infantry weapon throughout the duration of World War I was the M1891 Rifle, known as the "Mannlicher-Carcano" or simply "Carcano". It was manufactured in great numbers and in a number of variants from 1891 until the end of World War II, and it remained in service as a training rifle for the Italian Army and Police services up to the 1980s. The rifle achieved infamy in its short carbine version (seen in the image below) as the weapon used by Lee Harvey Oswald to assassinate President John F. Kennedy in 1963.

Fucile ("Mannlicher-Carcano") Modello 1891 (carbine version)

The Carcano was a rugged and reliable weapon fed by a 6-round en-bloc clip similar to that used by the US M1 Garand in World War II, shortening the reloading process considerably. Chambered in 6.5x52mm, it was accurate up to 500 yards in theory, but mediocre cartridges with substandard powder caused reliability and stopping power issues, which led to an attempted replacement of the cartridge in years between World War I and World War II.

The main battle rifle of the United States during World War I, the M1903 Springfield, remained in service throughout World War II, when it was carried into battle by the United States Marine Corps in the Pacific. Due to its accuracy, it also saw extensive use as a scoped sniper rifle and remains a popular sportsman's weapon in America to this day. Chambered in the specially-developed .30-06 cartridge (the same used later in the M1 Garand and scores of other weapons, and to this day one of the most widely used civilian game cartridges due to its power and excellent ballistics), it was loaded with a 5-round stripper clip and accurate up to 900 yards (with an effective range twice that). Extremely popular with the troops due to its high performance and virtual indestructibility, it suffered from some failures due to soldiers allegedly mistaking captured 7.92 Mauser cartridges for .30-06.

M1903 Springfield Rifle

The Mauser Gewehr M1898 was the spiritual son of the 1888 "commission rifle" developed for the German Army, which set the standard for bolt-action rifles that all other great powers attempted (with varying degrees of success) to copy. The M98 rifle was chambered in 7.92x54mm Mauser and was fed by a 5-round en-bloc clip, which was copied by the Italian Army for their Carcano Rifle. In the hands of a skilled marksman, it could hit targets consistently at 500 yards and was accurate at up to 1,000 with optics. Remodeled in a shorter, carbine version, the M98 would continue in service as the main rifle of the German Army. Like the Lee-Enfield, it is still in use in several conflict zones today due to its ruggedness and high performance. Its sportier cousin, the Mauser M98 Magnum, is still manufactured and is a popular big game rifle. Its smooth bolt and en-bloc clip allowed it to achieve up to 15 aimed shots per minute.

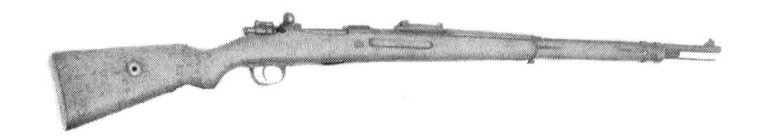

Mauser Gewehr M1898

The main service rifle of the Austro-Hungarian Empire was the Mannlicher 1895. Unlike the other rifles fielded by the Great Powers in World War I, it did not feature a conventional bolt action but instead employed a "straight pull" bolt, requiring the user to simply pull the bolt back and let it snap forward rather than lifting it up, pulling it back, and sliding it forward and back down again. This meant that the Mannlicher could manage upwards of 30 shots a minute, including reloads. The Mannlicher carried 5 rounds of 8x50mm ammunition in an en-bloc clip and was accurate to 400 yards. It was a reasonably reliable weapon, but the straight pull bolt was more prone to malfunction than the bolt action when subjected to dirt and user mismanagement, and as such it acquired a reputation for being more finicky than other rifles despite functioning well with proper maintenance.

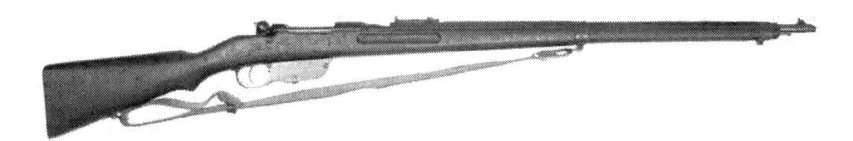

Mannlicher M1895

During World War I, pistols were issued almost exclusively to officers and occasionally some senior NCOs, but rankers also purchased or plundered them on occasion. Some specialist units (tank crews and machine-gunners) were occasionally equipped with sidearms, but as a general rule they were weapons for officers only. As such, there was a bewildering amount of pistols in different calibers and from different manufacturers available, as officers frequently purchased what would best suit their own requirements. It was not uncommon for British officers to possess Belgian or even German pistols, and vice versa, but each army had standard-issue sidearms.

The main sidearm of the British Imperial and Commonwealth armies was the venerable Webley Mk IV revolver. Originally introduced in 1887, the revolver had seen service all over the globe and was battle-tested and incredibly reliable. It fired six massive .455 cartridges, a round even larger than the famous .45 ACP, and it packed enough "stopping power" to drop an assailant dead in his tracks, a crucial feature in the close confines of trench warfare. This led to the revolver being issued to a number of specialist frontline troops, including trench raiders, the equivalent of the German *sturmtruppen* (Storm Troopers) that spearheaded infantry assaults. The Webley featured an extremely simple mechanism and very few moving parts, making it "trench-proof". Although weighty at over 2 pounds unloaded and capable of firing less shots before reloading than a semi-automatic pistol, it remained a favorite with soldiers, despite being slower to reload as well.

Webley Mk IV Revolver

The main sidearm of French Army Officers (including pilots) of the period was the MAS 1892, sometimes known as the Lebel 1892. The Lebel was a well-constructed firearm which, like most revolvers, possessed very few moving parts and thus was less prone to stoppages or malfunctions than some of the early semi-automatic pistols (although the open cylinder could foul with mud ort dirt). However, its 8mm cartridge was severely underpowered compared to other military sidearms of the time, making it equivalent to a slightly less powerful .32 ACP round. Although capable of penetrating bone (including the skull) at close ranges, it suffered from extremely poor ballistics at medium range, compromising its accuracy. Its weak stopping power also made it a rather poor choice as a weapon of last resort, since its caliber made it more suitable to a police weapon than a military pistol.

Manufacture d'Armes de Saint-Etienne Modele 1892 Revolver

Russia's main pistol throughout both World War I and World War II (during which it was supplemented but not wholly replaced by the semi-automatic Makarov) was the Nagant M1895. Firing six shots in 7.62x38mmR, the Nagant Revolver was unique among service sidearms in World War I in that it was offered in two versions: single and double-action. A double-action pistol allowed a trigger pull to both cock the hammer, rotate the cylinder and fire the shot, whereas a single-action pistol had to have the hammer cocked back by hand (or fanned, à la gunslinger) before the trigger could be pulled. The more expensive double-actions were issued to officers, while the single-actions went to other ranks. Like virtually all Russian military hardware, the Nagant was virtually indestructible and would fire despite being subjected to vast amounts of dirt and abuse. It remained in use with some Russian security forces until as recently as 2009, when it was finally retired after over a century of loyal service.

Nagant M1895 Revolver

The Glisenti Model 1910 was the main sidearm of the Italian Army in World War One, replacing the previously issued Bodeo 1889 Revolver. Unlike other pistols on this list, the Glisenti had a very limited life, being in service from 1910 to 1925. It fired the 9mm Glisenti, an underpowered version of the German 9x19mm parabellum (still in use in military and police sidearms all over the world). Although it could fit 7 rounds in its box magazine, the underpowered 9mm Glisenti had poor ballistic performance and was not effective as a military cartridge. The pistol itself was hounded by a large number of reliability problems, chiefly due to its large number of moving parts, some of which tended to come loose after repeat shots. It also possessed an extremely rudimentary safety, which led to a high number of accidental discharges.

Pistola Automatica Glisenti Modello 1910

The main sidearm of the United States Army during World War I, World War II, the Korean War and the Vietnam War until it was finally retired in the 1980s (despite widespread complaints from the military establishment), the "1911" is considered by many to be the greatest semi-automatic pistol ever produced. It still remains in use by many armies and security forces across the globe, and it is a favorite among private owners, both in its original configuration and in subsequently modified variants. The 1911 was chambered with the powerful .45 ACP cartridge and could fit 7 rounds in its magazine plus an eighth in the barrel. Its mechanism was simple and rugged, making it easy to clean and maintain and incredibly reliable. The pistol was in huge demand, so much so that the U.S. was forced to supplement it with large numbers of its former service revolver.

Colt M1911A1 Semi-Automatic Pistol

One of the most iconic semi-automatic pistols ever made and easily identifiable from countless war films, the Luger 1908 was adopted by the German Army to replace the *Reichsrevolver* prior to World War I. Chambered in 9x19mm parabellum, it could fit 8 rounds in its magazine and a further one in the chamber. Although less powerful than the Webley or 1911, its 9mm was nonetheless the perfect compromise between power and light recoil and is still the main caliber of most military, police and civilian sidearms worldwide. The Luger featured an unusual mechanism compared to other semi-automatic pistols, but it was nonetheless both reliable and popular, and it remained in service throughout the Second World War, when it was the preferred sidearm of Wehrmacht officers despite being phased out by the Walther 1938. It was also manufactured in a long-barreled "artillery" variant and issued to artillerymen with the option of a rifle stock for better aiming and a 32-round drum magazine, which turned it into a semi-automatic Personal Defense Weapon.

Pistole Parabellum 1908

The Roth-Steyr was part of a rather bizarre two-fold innovation designed to replace the Rast & Gasser 1898 as the side-arm of the Austro-Hungarian army, with cavalry units being meant to receive the Roth-Steyr and infantry regiments the Steyr M1912. However, military procurement issues and supply problems meant that the M1912 never saw widespread use in World War I, and while many in the army retained their Rast & Gasser revolvers, tens of thousands of Roth-Steyr pistols made their way to the front lines. The Roth-Steyr had the largest standard magazine capacity of any standard-issue sidearm during the war, fitting 10 8mm rounds inside its grip, and while the Roth-Steyr's cartridge was small, it was still effective. That said, the pistol was hampered by the fact that, unlike other sidearms, it did not load from a magazine but from a stripper clip, like a rifle. This diminished reloading speed somewhat, but it remained a preferable alternative to the Rast & Gasser, which was not top-break but had a loading gate into which shells had to be loaded individually in sequence.

Roth-Steyr M1907 Pistol

Chapter 2: Rapid Fire

Alongside artillery and rapid-firing bolt-action rifles, machine guns were the other great killers of World War I, and one of the main reasons that defensive firepower drastically outweighed offensive firepower until the introduction of man-portable Light Machine Guns during the second half of the war. The first modern machine gun was developed by the British inventor Sir Hiram Maxim, whose weapon was the first to use the gases of the cartridge's explosion to recoil the bolt and feed the next cartridge into the loading tray. It was thus the first to utilize a canvas belt and a water-cooling system. Most Heavy Machine Guns were cumbersome and difficult to relocate, required sizeable crews and, although a far cry from the prone-to-jamming, cumbersome Gatling Guns of the 19th century, still possessed impractical and finicky cooling and feeding systems. Naturally, advances made during the course of the war eventually led to finely tuned weapons, and the static nature of trench warfare meant that they rarely had to be moved from the apex of their precisely calculated interlocking arcs of fire anyway. As a result, heavy machine guns were employed during the war by each of the main belligerents.

Maxim

A Maxim gun aboard an American vessel in the 1890s

A simplified, stripped-down, lightweight version of the original Maxim Gun, the Vickers Gun was the workhorse of the British Army during the First World War. Exported to two dozen countries worldwide, it remained in service in foreign nations as a reliable and battle-tested design until the 1960s. Virtually indestructible, the Vickers could fire over a million rounds without a single stoppage, keeping up continuous fire for hours on end so long as the barrels (up to 100) were exchanged and it was handled by an experienced crew of 3 men (including a loader, gunner and commander). The Vickers could be moved if needed, but since it weighed around 45 lbs without its tripod, it worked best when locked in with a predetermined field of fire. It was effective up to 2000 yards and could lay down indirect suppressing fire up to double that distance, firing 500 rounds of the heavy .303 British cartridge a minute. Like virtually all heavy machine-guns of the period, it was a belt-fed design, and it used a water-cooling system, which was cumbersome since it required someone to cart around a tank of water and a tube if the weapon was moved. While this was far more effective than air for cooling the barrel, the gun's limitations ensured it was almost always used as a defensive weapon.

.303 Vickers Machine Gun

A Vickers machine gun operated by a crew with gas masks on at the Battle of the Somme

A design not unlike the Vickers Gun, the German MG08 came in two configurations: a standard sledge-mounted version and the lighter MG08/15, which was fitted with a bipod and a rifle stock and was designed as a man-portable, mobile fire-support platform. Despite these ameliorations, the MG08 still remained a water-cooled, belt-fed machine gun, so it was not popular with troops employed in an offensive capability. Another reliable weapon, though not as popular worldwide as the Vickers (or its own spiritual successor, the MG42), the MG08 remained in service among foreign nations until the 1960s. The gun itself weighed around 60 pounds, but the crew also had to carry a gallon of water and a heavy sledge mount which weighed a further 80 pounds in its standard configuration. Firing 600 rounds a minute of 7.92mm ammunition, the MG08 was effective to 2000 yards and could lay down suppressive fire to around 3500. It was operated by 4 men.

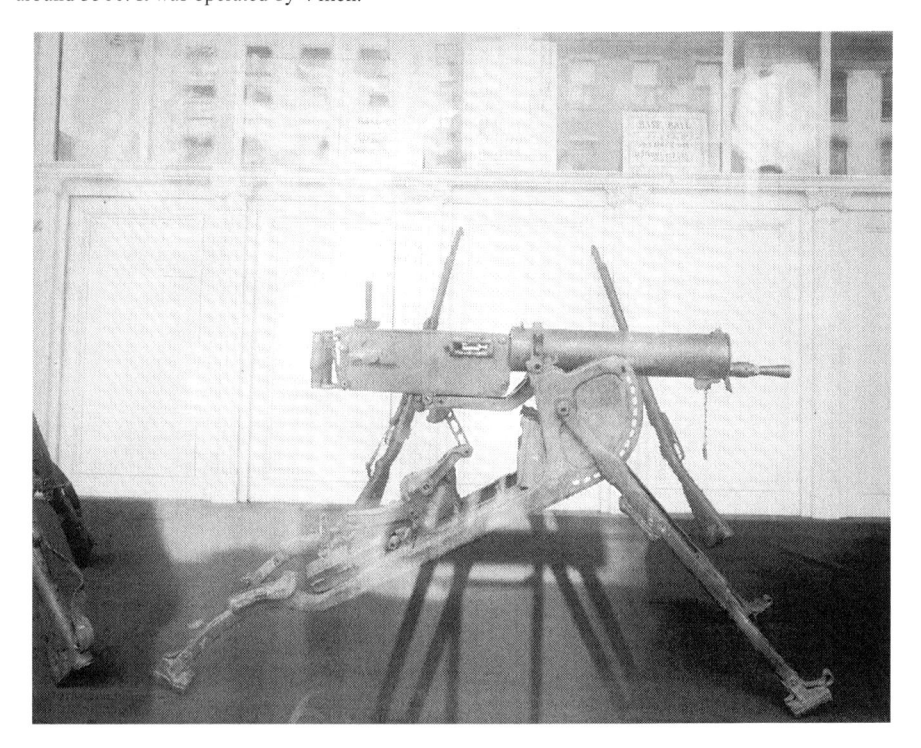

Maschinengewehr 08

A remarkably modern-looking design, France's Hotchkiss possessed several key features which made it unique among the heavy machine guns of the era. Although visually more "svelte" than other weapons such as the Vickers or MG08, the Hotchkiss actually weighed roughly the same (around 110 pounds). It was an air-cooled system, which theoretically made it more prone to overheating than other designs, but it compensated for this with a more rapid barrel-swapping mechanism that allowed it to continue providing suppressive fire for hours on end if needed. Its most distinctive feature was its somewhat unconventional feed system; instead of utilizing a canvas belt like other machine guns, it was fed via a 24-round metal strip which operated in a similar manner to the detachable magazines of later LMGs and assault rifles. The frequency with which these needed to be replaced made it somewhat less effective at providing sustained fire than other weapons, but it could still be made to fire rapidly in the hands of an experienced crew. Its range was comparable to that of other MGs of the period.

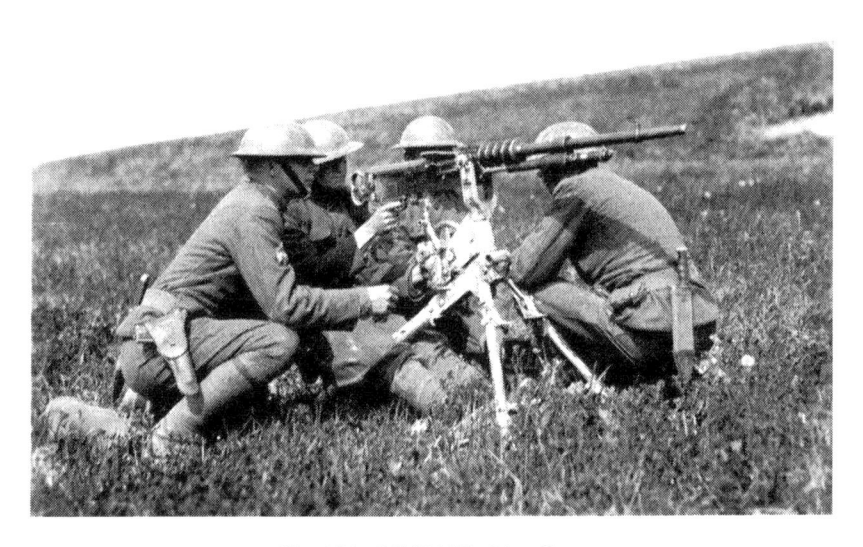

Hotchkiss M1914 Machine Gun

An extremely simplified "spiritual child" of the Maxim Gun, the Austrian M07/12 was mechanically less complex than both the Vickers and the MG08, and it weighed slightly less than either at around 90 pounds (with the sledge mount included). Crewed by 3 men (sometimes 4), the M07/12 proved to be an effective weapon, capable of between 500-600 rounds per minute and accurate to around 2000 yards. Like the MG08 and the Vickers, the Schwarzlose was water-cooled and belt-fed, but the simplicity of its design was also what made it least versatile; unlike its foreign brethren, it was not practical to reconfigure it for other uses, such as mounting it on aircraft or tanks. That said, like most machine guns of the era, it was a tough and reliable weapon.

M07/12

The most important of several Machine Guns which the Russian Army used during World War I, the PM M1910 was a licensed copy of Hiram Maxim's Maxim Gun (hence its name, which stands for Maxim Machine Gun Model 1910). It was chambered for the 7.62x54mmR Russian cartridge and came as a standard with its distinctive "wheelbarrow" mount and gunner shield. Being a Maxim Gun, it was belt-fed and water-cooled and accurate to around 2000 yards. Although the shield provided the gunner with some cover from enemy sniper fire, it also severely limited his field of vision, so in reality the weapon's accuracy was somewhat diminished. Like most Russian (and later Soviet) military technology, it was reliable, effective and virtually indestructible.

PM M1910 Machine Gun

Used alongside the Maxim Gun and several other Machine Guns by the Italian Army during the course of World War I, the Fiat-Revelli may have looked very similar to the various "Maxim-Descendants" fielded by other armies, but in practice it was very different. Water-cooled and weighing around 80 ponds with its tripod and water, it was fed not with a standard belt but with a unique – and impractical – system: a 50-round magazine which featured 10 different compartments, each filled with a Mannlicher-Carcano Rifle's standard clip. This arrangement, meant to ensure complete interchangeability between rifle and machine gun ammunition in practice, meant that magazines were extremely finicky, troublesome to reload, and susceptible to blockages, user-caused malfunction, and other problems. Although in theory capable of around 500 rounds a minute, Fiat-Revellis were almost never able to achieve these rates of fire in practice because their magazines plagued them with constant problems. An ill-fated design, it was retired after the end of World War I.

Mitragliatrice Fiat-Revelli Modello 1914

A spiritual successor to the Maxim Gun, America's M1917 was designed by legendary gunsmith John Moses Browning (creator of some of the most popular, effective and enduring firearms ever designed). It was a water-cooled, gas-blowback, belt-fed machine gun which fired up to 600 rounds a minute of .30-06 ammunition. Weighing 100 pounds with tripod, water and ammunition included, the Browning benefited from both an extremely gifted creator and a gap of several years' worth of technological development compared to most other weapons of the period. It was fielded in increasingly great numbers alongside the French Hotchkiss M1914, which it gradually phased out, but its cartridge was not capable of achieving similar ranges. It remained in service with the United States Marine Corps up to the Korean War.

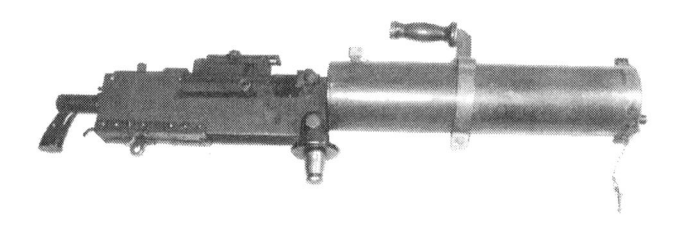

Browning M1917 Machine Gun

    Thus, the Machine Guns of the period, though accurate, effective and reliable, universally suffered from one key problem: they were extremely heavy. This meant that it was basically impossible to employ them in an offensive capacity, particularly over rugged terrain or the muddy, obstacle-strewn morass of no-man's-land, unless the weapon were crewed by supermen. To solve this problem during the war, a number of Light Machine Gun and Submachine Gun weapon designs were experimented with and eventually went into production, with the aim of allowing attacking troops and trench stormer units to equip the firepower of soldiers dug into a defensive position. By the end of the war, a number of highly effective designs were in service, with virtually all of the great powers using them except for Austria-Hungary and Russia (whose withdrawal from the war prevented the need for the immediate development of a weapon with those particular capabilities). These LMGs and SMGs were usually magazine-fed, air-cooled, and designed to be operated by one or at most two soldiers.

    One of the most iconic weapons of the early 20th century, the "Lewis Gun", was invented and designed in the United States but was adopted by the British Army as a source of light offensive firepower in 1915. Chambered in the standard .303 British rifle cartridge, it was fed by a "pan" magazine placed, unusually, on top of the barrel, and had a capacity of either 47 or 97 rounds. It was manufactured in various iterations, or Marks, throughout the course of the war, and issued to infantry squads. It had an effective range of up to 800 yards and could fire further in the suppressive fire role, but its key advantage was its relatively light weight at about 30 pounds, compared to heavy machine guns that weighed nearly 3 times more. It was also operated by one man, although he had a "second" who carried spare magazines for him and could change them if needed. Due to the design of the magazines, the machine gunner presented a very small profile when firing, making him a less conspicuous target. The Lewis Gun could also be fired standing or kneeling while gripping the bipod, although this feat took considerable strength.

A U.S. Marine testing a Lewis gun during the war

A major breakthrough in military technology that did not see deployment until the final year of the war when it was issued as the main weapon of the *Stosstruppen* (specially trained units designed to storm and capture enemy trenches), the Germans' MP1918 was a remarkable weapon. Chambered in the ever-popular 9mm parabellum (still a standard for military and law enforcement submachineguns), the MP1918 was light (weighing about 10 pounds loaded), compact, and capable of firing 32 rounds at 500 rounds per minute without reloading, making it lethal in the close confines of a trench. A first of its kind, it predated the more iconic "Tommy

Gun" by a number of years and proved to be very effective despite its somewhat limited use. Although its pistol cartridge was underpowered compared to that of an LMG, it was more than capable of clearing trenches at close quarters, a job for which long-range ballistics were unnecessary.

Maschinenpistole 1918

A German soldier holding one during the war

The Fusil Mitrailleure Modele 1915 CSRG, unofficially known as the Chauchat, was the French answer to the Lewis Gun. It was the most widely produced automatic weapon of the war, manufactured not just extensively for French use but also for the American Expeditionary Force and for the Belgian Army. Chambered in 8mm Lebel, it was accurate to over 200 yards and fed by a 20-round box magazine. In theory, the Chauchat, which at 20 pounds was one of the lightest LMGs of the time, was the answer to a soldier's prayer as a source of effective offensive firepower in a relatively compact, lightweight package, but in reality, the Chauchat was almost universally reviled. Its chief problem, which caused a vast number of stoppages, was the fact that its "half-moon" magazines were open on the side, thereby exposing cartridges to the elements. When dirt and mud inevitably became gummed into the works as the weapon was hauled through no-man's-land, it caused malfunctions. The Chauchat would also "lock up" if fired for too long due to heat expansion, its sights were improperly formed, and it was virtually uncontrollable at medium to long range.

"Chauchat" Light Machine Gun

Designed by one of Italy's most highly regarded gunsmiths, the Beretta M1918 was a remarkably advanced weapon for its time. It was used by the "truppe d'assalto" as a replacement for their retro-fitted Villar Perosa Machine Guns, a 9mm magazine-fed aircraft weapon that had proved virtually useless in its original role but had been found to be effective as a shoulder-fired SMG. The M1918 fed from the top, an unusual design for a SMG, the reason being that this allowed gravity to eject the spent shell. Chambered in 9mm Glisenti, the M1918 was fed by a 25-round detachable box and, unusual for an SMG, was also equipped with a folding bayonet, an indication of its suggested use as a trench-storming weapon. Its introduction into service predated the German MP1918, making it the first general-service SMG.

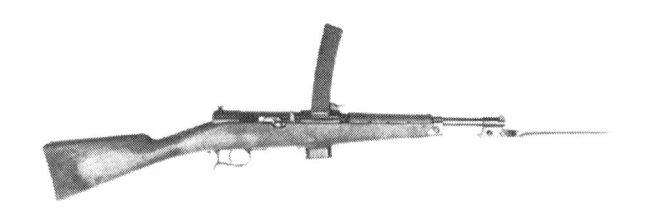

Beretta M1918

Another one of John Moses Browning's most inspired designs, the Browning Automatic Rifle (or BAR) was issued to American troops alongside the Chauchat, though initially in far smaller numbers. It was originally set to phase-out the problem-ridden French LMG, but the war ended before this occurred, in part because American soldiers were reluctant to let the Germans capture any of the weapons. An "Automatic Rifle" rather than a Light Machine Gun due to the relatively small size of its box magazine (20 rounds), it was nonetheless an extremely reliable, effective design which was popular with the soldiers. It was purchased by a large number of countries internationally, saw widespread use by the Army in World War II, and was still in service in Vietnam before being replaced by the M60 LMG. Weighing less than 20 pounds, it was easy to maneuver and could be fired effectively from the hip or shoulder. When fired from the prone position with its bipod, it was accurate to 1500 yards, and it could be fired in a suppressive capacity considerably further (up to 5000 yards), but due to the limited size of its magazine, this technique was not recommended. The BAR, like most weapons designed by John Browning, was well ahead of its time, extremely effective, remarkably problem-free, and virtually "soldier-proof", holding up to the stresses of trench warfare remarkably well. In essence, the BAR may be viewed as one of the earliest examples of an assault rifle, although it does not quite tick all the boxes to be officially classified as one.

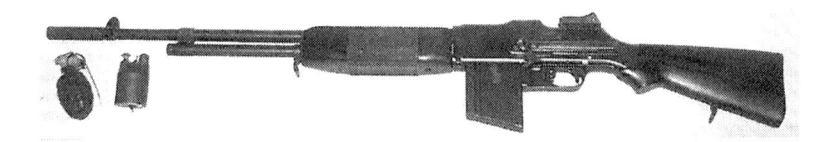

M1918 Browning Automatic Rifle

Chapter 3: The Steel Rain

In the second half of the 19th century, with the exception of some major conflicts (like the Crimean War and the American Civil War) between industrialized combatants, artillery had suffered something of a decline. Due to a number of reasons, it had gone from being the dominant arm in terms of raw killpower to something of a forgotten ancillary. To begin with, the wars that most of the great powers had been involved in had been wars over colonial expansion fought by the likes of Britain, France, and Germany in places like Africa. These small wars usually shared two key features: a technological imbalance between invaders and the local forces, and the need for small, highly mobile units. Because of this, there was little need for heavy artillery, as it was both slow-moving and of little use against enemies who tended to cover ground very quickly to get to close quarters and whose fortifications were antiquated enough not to require modern siege guns. Additionally, the technological advantages in rifle range and accuracy, as well as the introduction of machine guns, meant that infantry battalions could now engage the enemy effectively at four to five times the range they had been able to only half a century earlier. This meant that the artillery, which even in small-scale conflicts had acted as a force multiplier and long-range killer, had become redundant in this particular type of conflict.

Nevertheless, the development of guns and of the science of gunnery continued throughout the 19th century, and a number of important technological innovations took place in the years leading up to the outbreak of the war. Furthermore, countries like Britain, France, Germany and Russia had not been obliged by budgetary constraints to downsize on arms and equipment deemed obsolete or unnecessary for the small wars they were fighting. As a result, military expenditures still commanded a large part of their budgets, and they were able to stockpile and develop arms for the future. The Franco-Prussian War of 1871, as well as the growing belligerence of Prussia (and later Germany) as a power poised for aggressive expansion, persuaded policy-makers in Europe of the need to maintain a large artillery arm for the war among great powers that they believed was inevitable, and the subsequent arms race for a future European war led the artillery to swell to hitherto unseen numbers. By the outbreak of World War I, there were more men (almost a million) serving in the Royal Artillery than there were in the Royal Navy.

At the beginning of the 19th century, cannons had been like giant muzzle-loading shotguns. The powder charge was placed in the barrel from the front, then a round (later conical) ball or shell was placed atop it, and then wadding was added to ensure the force of the explosion did not escape around the shell's edges. The powder was then ignited with a flintlock or fuse by a gunner. This whole process was laborious and limited the accuracy of artillery, but in the mid-19th century, a number of key innovations changed the entire face of gunnery. There were four major developments which transformed guns from those of the Napoleonic Era into those which, with some modifications, are still used to this day. These were: rifling, breech-loading, stronger barrels, and hydro-pneumatic recoil absorption mechanisms. Later, "cartridge" shells which functioned in the same way as giant rifle cartridges were introduced, but initially, "modern" artillery still had a separate powder charge and high-explosive shell. Additionally, the quality of explosive propellants also improved, allowing for far more powerful charges which could deliver ordnance at vastly increased ranges. Three of these innovations (rifling, breech-loading, stronger barrels) were introduced in the British-made Armstrong Gun in 1858, but it was not until 1897, less than 20 years before the outbreak of World War I, that all four were incorporated into the

French Model 75 field gun.

The French Model 75

Rifling had been present in military issue small arms since the British formed the Experimental Corps of Riflemen in 1800, but the industrial machines necessary to carve rifling (a spiralling system of grooves and ridges that imparted a spin on the round, making it less susceptible to windage and therefore capable of being vastly more accurate at long range) did not exist until the mid-1800s. The problem of how to ensure that none of the explosive force of the propellant was wasted by escaping around the shell was solved by coating it with a thin veneer of lead. Since the lead was soft, it could grip the rifling without wearing it away, ensuring a perfect fit with the barrel. Perfected industrial output techniques also ensured that all shells were exactly the same size, unlike what might have been the case earlier in the century. Moreover, Armstrong guns also featured a bore which functioned somewhat like a shotgun's "choke", being narrower at the exit of the barrel than it was at the breech. This meant that in the final few inches of the barrel, part of the outer lead coating was peeled off the shell, both centering the round and improving its performance over long distances.

The other major innovation, breech-loading, had been tried before but never with particular success. Essentially, the round or cartridge was loaded via the bottom or breech of the barrel rather than rammed in from the front, which substantially increased reload speed, but having the breech have a trap or loading gate rather than the entire barrel being cast from one solid piece significantly weakened the whole gun, which tended to blow apart if subjected to heavy loads. However, improvements in steel workmanship and metallurgical techniques used in heavy machinery meant that arsenals were able to construct guns that could handle a far higher amount of explosive force without any mechanical failure. This was not just in the breech area but also in the barrel, which tended to blow apart in solid-cast pieces after repeat firings when subjected to the internal pressures of high-explosive. A solution to this was found by fitting a number of tubes of progressively smaller diameters within each other to form the barrel by heating them so that they expanded and then allowing them to contract around the previous tube by cooling. This meant that the metal was constantly attempting to return to its original shape, making it far stronger in resisting outward explosive force.

Armstrong guns had been provided with a carriage that allowed the gun to roll back into place once it had fired, unlike previous cannons, which needed to be manually moved back into place after every shot had slewed it out of position, significantly reducing rates of fire. However, the system used by the Armstrong guns was still rudimentary and did not allow for maximum efficiency. It was the French Army that first solved this problem by developing a hydro-pneumatic recoil dampener for field artillery. What this ensured was that wheeled artillery (unlike mortars, where the force was directed downwards) no longer rolled backwards with every blast; instead, the barrel of the gun itself moved backwards on a series of hydraulic levers before returning to its original position, thus exhausting the recoil of the piece while the carriage itself remained immobile. This (as well as the introduction of cased "cartridge" shells) increased the number of shots an artillery piece could fire by several orders of magnitude. At the start of the 19th century, artillery had been able to achieve 4-5 rounds per minute, but by 1900, guns could fire 15 rounds per minute as standard or up to 30 at double-time, rates comparable to most rifles of the period. Field pieces like the French Model 75 could fire high explosive shells up to a range of 5 miles away, and within a few years, all great powers could field comparable guns by the thousands.

An Armstrong gun in use during the American Civil War

Of course, these standard artillery pieces had nothing on the innovations that came during the war, especially the advances brought about by the Germans. Chiefly due to the strategic imperative behind the Schlieffen Plan, which predicated a lightning advance into the French heartland and on to Paris, the Germans required speed, as had been achieved during the Franco-Prussian War. This meant it was necessary to reduce the great fortifications the French were building precisely to guard against such an outcome. To do so rapidly, the Germans needed bigger and more powerful guns than the French could even imagine, and thus were born the notorious superheavy artillery pieces of World War I.

Among the most famous of these, fielded from the very beginning of 1914, were the 16-inch calibre guns nicknamed "Big Bertha" by the Allies. Manufactured by Krupp, the "Big Berthas" (of varying class) fired a shell weighing over a ton more than 8 miles, and while this enormous round required significantly more time to load than standard field artillery shells, it inflicted vast destruction upon concrete fortifications not reinforced with steel. Shots from the Big Bertha destroyed Belgian forts with the utmost ease in the opening days of the war, including one with a single shot that penetrated the fort's ammunition magazine on the first discharge and blew it apart. Though the French forts (which included steel reinforcements) were able to fare better against the Big Berthas, they remained a much-feared weapon throughout the war.

A Big Bertha

The Germans' Gamma-Gerät (Gamma-device), a predecessor of Big Bertha

Massive though the Big Berthas were, they were not the largest or most modern artillery pieces developed in an attempt to break the bloody deadlock of the Western Front. In response to the German "fortbusters," by 1916 the French had developed superguns of their own (although the demand for conventional ordnance and artillery meant that these were not deployed before the end of the war). The first one, the Obusier de 520 modele 1916 railroad gun, was not delivered until late 1917. A railroad gun, as the name suggests, was a cannon mounted on a specially constructed railway carriage, as nothing but a train possessed the sheer power to shift such a mountainous mass of metal. The Modele 1916 weighed over 26 tons, was nearly 100 feet long, and had a 35 foot barrel, which allowed it to fire 3,000 pound 20-inch shells over 18,000 yards (nearly 10 miles). Although it had a hydraulic recoil dampening mechanism, it still shunted the heavy steel carriage and its own 26-ton bulk more than a yard backwards, despite the use of a series of steel clamps which latched onto the tracks to increase friction. Due to the massive weight of its shells, the Modele 1916 was capable of firing only one round every five minutes, but whatever was on the receiving end of its massive mouth would certainly be aware of it.

CRADLE SLIDING RECOIL MOUNT FOR FRENCH 520-MM. HOWITZER.

The Obusier de 520 modele 1916 railroad gun

The Germans themselves continued to develop bigger and more powerful superheavy artillery pieces, and the ones they produced in the final years of the war put even the Modele 1916 to shame. The most notorious of these were the Paris Guns, or Kaiser Wilhelm Guns. Specific details about the legendary Paris Guns are sketchy, not least because as the Allies advanced inexorably towards Germany they were dismantled and completely destroyed, but from photographic and written evidence, it's known that they were roughly 100 feet long, weighed around 250 tons, and were capable of firing a relatively small 220 pound shell. Paris Guns were also maintenance-heavy and were relatively inaccurate. This all suggests that the Paris Guns were not particularly effective in practical terms, but what made the Paris Guns truly remarkable was their range. They were capable of hitting a (large) target at a staggering 80 miles away, 10 times the range of the mighty Big Bertha. These guns were used in the latter half of the war as a final attempt to break the will of the French population by firing directly where German troops could not hope to reach: the heart of Paris itself. The Paris Guns rained down an unknown number of shells on the French capital, shocking the local citizens to the extent that many assumed they were being targeted by a Zeppelin bomber since the gun was so far away that it was impossible to hear it firing. Ultimately, the Paris Guns were unsuccessful as a propaganda weapon in breaking the French civilian population's spirit, but they are a testament to German wartime engineering and the sheer ingenuity Kaiser Wilhelm's scientists were able to harness to the purpose of building machines of destruction. In fact, the range of the Paris Guns was so amazing that when they were fired, the gunners had to take into account the Coriolis Effect (the rotation of the Earth) because their shots were actually launched into the stratosphere. They marked the first weapons to launch a man-made object to that altitude.

A Paris Gun

The British also developed their own superguns, but in their case these guns were mounted primarily on Monitors, shallow-draft ships designed to lie close to the shore and support operations by firing inland, which they did to great effect along the Belgian coast. The British monitors of the Abercrombie and Erebus class, designed and constructed between 1915 and 1916, were armed with two superguns: the BL 15 inch Mark I. These guns fired a 2000 pound shell over 30,000 yards (about 18 miles) and were thus capable of delivering ordnance on target far inland despite being fired from a seaborne platform.

The abilities of these superweapons, as well as the thousands of pieces of conventional field artillery deployed by the various great powers during the war, would have been unable to fire with such devastating effectiveness without improvements in the science of gunnery. Throughout the war, the combatants could launch tens of thousands of shells within just a few hours during preliminary bombardments which preceded major attacks, something that 19th century commanders would have found inconceivable. For most of the 19th century, aside from mortars, artillery still fired in a flat or slightly arched trajectory at targets within their line of sight. This remained the case until the late 1880s, when the German Army created the lining plane, which allowed gunners to target more effectively. However, this method was entirely superseded a few years later by an optical sight, the Panoramic Telescope or Dial Sight, which allowed gunners to rapidly establish the azimuth and train their pieces with greater precision. Techniques continued to improve dramatically in the years leading up to the war and in the opening stages of the conflict when aerial photography allowed for the pinpointing of targets not in line of sight. It took a while to adapt these techniques effectively to battlefield situations, as the fact that rounds could now be delivered at such vast distances severely affected initial accuracy when not firing in perfect conditions. However, by the final years of the war, field artillery was capable of "firing off the map" by utilizing a series of grid coordinates, thereby allowing gunners to rapidly deliver barrages with pinpoint accuracy. This technique has changed little in the past century as it continues to prove itself effective and efficient.

Chapter 4: Unstoppable Juggernauts

One of the most important breakthroughs in military technology associated with World War I, and certainly the one that continues to capture the public imagination, was the introduction of a war machine that came to dominate the face of land battles throughout most of the 20th century: the tank. As a concept, it was not revolutionary; in fact, it harkened back to classical antiquity and to the Middle Ages, such as the covered battering rams and *testudos* which had made frequent appearances on ancient battlefields. In essence, it was designed to solve the age-old problem of protecting infantry from enemy projectiles while remaining mobile.

The development of both modern artillery and machine guns, as well as the stalemate engendered by heavy fortifications and entrenchments, had hamstrung the mobility of infantry and cavalry and also left them both utterly vulnerable to defensive firepower. Since they were incapable of replying in kind, the tank was designed to bridge that gap. The tank's armor, thick enough to withstand lateral fragmentation from exploding shells (although not direct hits) also made it virtually invulnerable to enemy rifle and machine gun fire, and its large tread meant that it could bridge trenches which would, at the very least, have delayed infantry substantially. As for the barbed wire entanglements and obstacles that severely delayed infantry and exposed them to enemy fire, tanks could simply drive right through it.

Various armies had flirted with the concept of a tank prior to World War I, but advances in metallurgical techniques (allowing for suitably solid and relatively lightweight armor) and in mechanical engineering (which allowed for the construction of a powerful engine capable of driving such a mass) finally made its development and deployment possible, as did the development of treaded track (initially for agricultural use in tractors). It was the British (at the instigation of Winston Churchill) who pioneered the "landship", but the French soon followed suit with their own designs. Ironically, it was the Germans, who would subsequently become famous for their panzers and blitzkrieg warfare, who were late in taking up the idea. During World War I, the Germans continued to rely on other techniques, and they produced less than two dozen models for battlefield use.

The tanks of World War I, revolutionary (and initially terrifying) as they were, had their limitations. A standard tank would literally consume its own weight in spare parts, and they were painfully slow compared to more modern iterations. They were also lightly armed – usually with machine guns or light guns at most – and some poorly designed models tended to "ditch" themselves, sometimes irretrievably, in wider trenches. However, as a mobile bastion for infantry to shelter behind in the advance, and as a psychological weapon, they were significant.

The most iconic tank of World War I, the Mark I (which later went through several iterations, although only Mark I-IV saw combat during the war), was employed by a number of armies. The Mark I was produced by a specially designed government committee with the full cooperation of all services and British industry, resulting in a cohesive and practical whole. Over 30 feet long and weighing just under 30 tons, the Mark I came in two versions: a "male" (armed with side-mounted turret guns) and a "female" that didn't have the guns. Crewed by 8 men, it could achieve the rather unspectacular speed of 4 miles per hour, and its 60-gallon tank gave it an operational radius of just under 24 miles thanks to its thirsty Daimler-Knight 6-cylinder, 16 liter straight petrol engine, which generated 105 horsepower. The tank's armament was two 6-pounder light guns for the male, plus three .303 Hotchkiss machine guns, while the female version carried four .303 Vickers machine guns instead of artillery and a .303 Hotchkiss machine gun. The Mark I-IV, of which over 2,000 models were produced for wartime action, saw service at the Somme, Fleurs-Corciette and Amiens on the Western Front, and during both battles of Gaza in North Africa against Turkish forces.

Mark I-IV Tank

The British tanks suffered from a number of issues, not least of which was the development of armor-piercing bullets by the Germans in the latter part of the war, and due to mechanical failure or enemy action, only a third of them usually reached enemy positions. However, those that did reach that far almost always contributed significantly to a final victory. A thousand were ordered for later British use, but the end of the conflict brought wartime production to a standstill.

France's initial forays into tank design were not an unqualified success. Unlike the concerted efforts made by the British Armed Forces and the various private companies involved in production, the French initially operated at cross-purposes, thus producing a number of ill-starred early efforts which suffered from some serious design flaws. By 1917, however, thanks primarily to the efforts made by Renault to come up with a successful design, the French were able to field significant numbers of small, agile, and lightly armored tanks. The French envisioned having these tanks operate as a "swarm", a tactic unlike the British but one that was adopted by the Americans, who also purchased and manned the Renault FT. Crewed by just two men, the Renault FT was a little over 15 feet long and weighed just over 6 tons (a third of the Mark I-IVs). It had an operational range of around 40 miles thanks to its 4.5 liter, 4-cylinder Renault petrol engine. The Renault FT was significantly faster than the British tanks, allowing it to operate with a tactical agility reminiscent of what the previous century's cavalry had been able to achieve, and it was also mechanically more reliable. It was far less heavily armed, however, as its two variants being either one single light gun or a single .303 machine gun. Designed to be an agile, fast-hitting screen for maneuverable warfare, over 3000 were produced for use by the French and Americans.

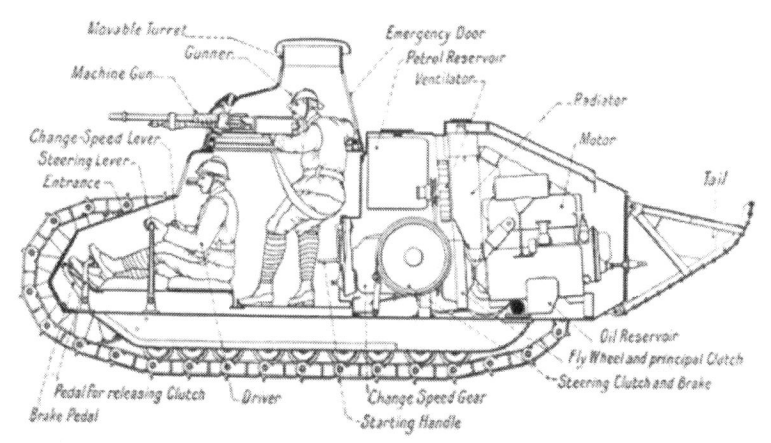

DIAGRAMMATIC SECTION OF A FRENCH LIGHT (OR "MOSQUITO") TANK.

Renault FT "Mosquito" Light Tank

Unlike the remarkable advances the Germans made developing zeppelins, aircraft, heavy artillery and machine guns, they were reluctant to develop tanks and never considered doing so until they found themselves on the receiving end of tank assaults at the Somme. The final product of their efforts was the A7V, envisioned more as an armored troop transport than as an offensive vehicle. Only 20 were eventually produced for battlefield service, but the Germans also employed captured Allied tanks. They saw action on the Western Front at Villers-Bretonneux, where they faced off Against allied tanks in the first tank-on-tank battle, and in other engagements, including the Battles of Aisne and the Marne.

The A7V

The A7V was over 20 feet long and weighed 33 tons, more than even the heaviest Mark I-IVs. It also carried a relatively heavy 57mm gun and six machine guns, and it was powered by two engines: Daimler-Benz 4-cylinders capable of 100 horsepower apiece. This gave it an operational range of between 20-50 miles depending on terrain and fuel tank size, and a top speed of 9 miles per hour on road and 4 miles per hour cross-country. The A7V carried a full complement of 18 men, and in many ways it was a superior machine to its equivalent, the British Mark I-IV, since it was capable of slightly greater speeds and more heavily armed. However, German reluctance to use tanks as a viable battlefield advantage meant that the Germans were never able to field anywhere near the number of vehicles the Allies were.

Chapter 5: Airplanes

While the war quickly ground to a halt in its first few months, the skies above the Western Front became increasingly busy. The great powers had already been acquiring aircraft for potential uses, but given that aerial warfare had never been a major component of any conflict, it's understandable that few on either side had any idea what the planes were capable of doing. Furthermore, at the start of the war, all sides' aircraft were ill-equipped for combat mostly because the idea that planes might somehow fight was still a novel one, and the adaptations had not yet been developed that would allow the aerial battles later in the war.

As a result, aircraft were used almost entirely for reconnaissance early on, allowing generals to gain unprecedented levels of information about enemy movements. Such intelligence allowed the French to counter German movements in what became the First Battle of the Marne, ending Germany's hopes for victory through the Schlieffen plan. Similarly, in the east, German planes were vital in tracking, encircling and destroying Russian forces at Tannenberg.

Some armies, such as the French, saw air intelligence as a strategic matter, with aircraft capable mainly of identifying enemy forces before battle and contributing to advanced preparations. The Germans, on the other hand, believed that aircraft could provide tactical information once battle had commenced. Pilots such as Oswald Boelcke, Germany's first great aerial officer, would fly over enemy positions in two-seat aircraft with a spotter in the back, identifying Allied positions and using colored lights to direct the fire of artillery on the ground.

Of course, spotting took on great importance because of the growing range and power of artillery. Much of the fire from the great guns was aimed indirectly since the gunners could not see their targets and thus relied on intelligence from others to direct them. Maps of enemy-held territory were often woefully inadequate to start with, and with the need to know where moving enemy formations were positioned, the business gained an added complexity, but aircraft could cut through this by providing up-to-date intelligence on enemy positions and sending it back to the gun batteries which were lobbing shells over their own front lines.

At the same time, the use of aircraft to carry weapons began early on. Bombs were dropped on Paris in August 1914, and zeppelins bombed Belgian forces as the Germans advanced on Liège. On the other side, British pilots destroyed a Zeppelin on the ground at Düsseldorf. This was bombing at its most simple; the explosives were kept on hooks on the side of the machines and dropped by a crew member by hand. These small forays into aerial bombardment barely even hinted at the bombing campaigns to come.

Picture of a Zeppelin during the war

Picture of a crater left by a zeppelin bomb in Paris during the war

The Zeppelins, slow and large as they were, proved to be easy targets for fire from the ground, so they were too vulnerable for reconnaissance in the warzone. Instead, they were used for the task of bombing England's eastern ports and London in an attempt to disrupt military supplies. This left the planes to fight for control of the skies over the Western front. From the start, pilots from opposing sides tried to take each other out and ensure their side's advantage in aerial intelligence, but since the machines were not equipped with weapons themselves, pilots initially carried hand weapons to fire from the cockpit or try to get above the enemy and drop projectiles. Flying at speeds up to 70 miles per hour and heights of up to 4,000 feet, these were not the fast-moving dogfights that would become a staple of later warfare, but by the standards of the time, these were exhilarating heights and speeds.

In rushing winds, men fought to steady themselves and draw a bead on the enemy in what started out as little more than sport between like-minded fliers but soon turned into a bitter battle for survival. It quickly became apparent that changes would be needed in the battle for aerial supremacy, and two different styles of plane emerged. On the one hand, there were the traditional two-seater crafts used for reconnaissance and the emerging art of bombing, with one man piloting while another took observations or dropped munitions. On the other hand, there were the fast single-seater scouts, designed to patrol the skies, chase away enemy planes and provide their side with aerial superiority. These new scouting planes needed forward firing guns so that the pilots could aim and fire without taking their attention off where they were going, but this created a problem, as guns mounted on the body of the plane were prone to shooting off their own propellers and taking them out before they could do any damage to the enemy, while those mounted high above the body were hard to aim, fire and unjam.

The French were the first to tackle the problem by designing a propeller reinforced with steel wedges to deflect the bullets, but it was far from a perfect solution. The bullets could still damage the propellers, and by sending them flying in every direction, the mechanism risked deflecting a bullet back at the pilot. In 1915, the German airforce solved this problem and thus immediately gained a technological advantage over their opponents. Dutch engineer Anthony Fokker's interrupter gear stopped the gun from firing when a propeller blade was in front of it, but the gear allowed it to keep firing in the split seconds in between. This meant that for the first time, planes could be mounted with an automatic weapon that would shoot straight ahead, targeted in the same direction that the pilot was guiding the plane, and which did not risk shooting off the plane's own propeller or filling the pilot's face with rogue lead.

Fokker

As a result, starting in July 1915 with the Fokker E.I plane, German aircraft became war machines in their own right. Fokker's new aircraft was not only mounted with a superior weapon, it could also go faster and higher than most craft then in the skies. For the next six months, Germany had aerial superiority thanks to these planes, and aircraft production accelerated quickly. Having entered the war with a few hundred aircraft, Germany produced another 1,350 in 1914 and rising to 19,750 in 1917, a 15-fold increase in just three years.

Picture of a Fokker E.1

The tactics of aerial combat were also developing fast, and with its consequences of victory or death, fighting provided a good motive to learn better approaches as soon as possible. Oswald Boelcke, who without official permission had taken Fokker's plane for its first real outing, took the lead in developing the tactics that would make the Fokker plane invaluable. Staying on the German side of the lines, he used clouds and the glare of the sun to disguise his approach before shooting enemy planes down with short, accurate bursts of fire at close range. He paid attention not just to the workings of his machine but to those of his opponents, learning the design and limitations of captured Allied planes and determining the capabilities of their guns and where their blind spots lay. He also collaborated with the German anti-aircraft gunners on the ground, who provided him with warning shots when he was in danger and covering fire when he was under attack.

Boelcke

One of Boelcke's colleagues, Max Immelmann, added a sophisticated high speed maneuver to the German arsenal. The Immelmann turn, the first true air-to-air tactical maneuver, allowed the Fokker planes to attack their enemies again and again in quick succession, adding to their dominance as long as the enemy flew inferior planes. Its success helped earn its inventor his nickname "The Eagle of Lille," but this superiority only lasted until the following spring, when the Allied Powers developed and installed their own version of the Fokker technology. With that adaptation, the maneuver that had given Germans dominance now became a hazard to its own users.

Immelmann

Furthermore, Boelcke and Immelmann introduced the formation that has been the basis of fighter groups ever since: the pair of fighters. Boelcke realized that hunting out targets required a dangerous amount of attention; after all, while he was focused on stalking a single plane, others could approach without him noticing it. This meant the tactics which brought him success were also putting his life in danger. He therefore teamed up with Immelmann, with the two guarding and protecting each other. The radios of the time were too heavy and cumbersome to install in an aircraft, so the pilots signaled to each other by waggling the wings of their planes, with Boelcke as the leader deciding when to attack and when to break off.

In January 1916, Immelmann and Boelcke, the first great heroes of aerial warfare, both received the Pour le Mérite awards, the highest honor in Germany, after shooting down their 8th enemy aircraft. They had become symbols of German dominance in the skies, but their planes, like those of their German comrades, were being used purely defensively, assigned to reconnaissance and spotter balloon squadrons to provide them with defense. They were out-shooting the Allies, preventing them from gaining advantages but not helping to push German troops forward.

1916 also saw a period in which technological advances gave the Allied Powers the upper hand. The Allies threw hundreds of pilots into supporting the bloody ground offensive on the Somme, and in doing so greatly supported their war effort. The British were hurling men and planes into the meat grinder, putting little effort into providing training and experience before they did so, but in the broader scope of the war, this was supporting their aims.

Later in 1916, the Germans regained the edge with the Albatros D.III plane, and the see-saw of military technological advantage swayed back and forth. Industrial programs were increasingly important when it came to providing both new technology and large amounts of material for aerial combat, and the Germans were not yet suffering from the shortages that would late hamper them.

The Albatros D.III

Boelcke's tactics were now fundamental for German military fliers. Pilots gained the advantage before they even entered combat, attacking from above with the sun to their backs. Shooting was in short bursts at close range, ignoring the instinct to fill the sky with a wild spray of bullets. When attacked, pilots did not run but turned towards their attackers, facing them head on to remove their advantage. It was an approach that required both calculation and daring, a perfect fit for men like Boelcke and the Red Baron, Manfred von Richthofen.

The Red Baron

Other innovations included the adoption of large formations of fighter aircraft. This started out as an Allied innovation to protect their planes from the technologically superior Fokkers, new models of which were now being produced. The Germans responded by forming squadrons of first 6 and then 14 planes, with Boelcke put in charge of a formation each time. It was on his suggestion that the German command formed the elite Jadgstaffeln units (or Jasta as they became known), large squadrons of top fliers whose purpose was to hunt Allied air formations and take them out of the skies. August 1916 saw the creation of the first two such formations: Jasta 1 under Hauptmann Zander and Jasta 2 under Boelcke himself. Such was his standing that he was allowed to hand pick his pilots, and while putting them together, Boelcke met young Lieutenant Manfred von Richthofen.

Eventually, Richthofen joined Boelcke's "Hunting Pack", and his reputation would eventually come to surpass that of his commander, but at the same time, it's only fair to point out that Richthofen's rise to prominence came in part because of the loss of the greats who had come before him. Death was common for fliers, and often terrible. There were no parachutes, and the best hope of surviving a damaged plane was a risky crash landing. If the plane caught fire then the pilot would often jump to his death rather than die in a cockpit inferno. These young officers were avoiding the now infamous horrors of trench warfare, but they faced their own sort of terror.

Indeed, Immelmann, who in the early days achieved as many victories as his flying partner, died when his machine fell apart in the air in 1916. Boelcke, after a hugely successful autumn with his enlarged squadron and new Albatros plane, died in October 1916 when he crashed into another plane while diving towards an Allied aircraft. With the deaths of Immelmann and Boelcke, Germany had lost her first great aerial heroes, but another was coming to take their place. No longer under Boelcke's tutelage, von Richthofen was emerging as a leading pilot in his own right, and by early 1917 von Richthofen's star was on the rise. On January 4, he had shot down his 16th plane, making him one of Germany's leading fliers and a popular hero at home. He was awarded the order *Pour le Mérite* for his achievements, and by the end of the month he was commanding his own squadron, Jasta 11. His instructions for his men were simple: "Aim for the man and don't miss him. If you are fighting a two-seater, get the observer first; until you have silenced the gun, don't bother about the pilot."

April 1917 was one of the most successful phases of the war for the Germans in the sky. The Red Baron and his men brought down dozens of British planes in what their opponents referred to as "bloody April," and in just five days from April 4-8, the British lost 75 planes, with 19 men killed, 13 wounded, and 73 reported missing. The most significant single engagement of this fighting came on April 28, when British flier Captain W. Leefe Robinson, a man who had earned the Victoria Cross for shooting down a zeppelin, led six Bristol F2B fighters of Number 48 Squadron across enemy lines. The Bristol was the great new hope of the Royal Flying Corps, a heavily armed two-seater plane with a forward firing Vickers machine-gun and a pair of Lewis guns operated by the observer in the rear seat. A sturdy, powerful plane, it held great promise for the British, but their unfamiliarity with it would lead to an unfortunate early outing. The Bristols had barely crossed the front line when five German Albatros planes, led by von Richthofen, descended upon them. The British might have fine new planes, but the Germans were familiar with their own machines and had the tactical advantage. Almost immediately, von Richthofen took out the first Bristol, sending it spinning towards the ground. A vicious dogfight ensued, during which three more of the Bristols were shot down, and the last two, one piloted by Leefe Robinson, staggered away. Nonetheless, the captain's plane was too badly damaged to make it back to the British lines, forcing him to land his bullet-torn machine in German territory, where he was captured and spent the rest of the war a prisoner. Von Richthofen had turned the first outing of the glorious new British flying machine into a total disaster.

Including the engagement on April 28, the Red Baron himself shot down 21 British planes that month, and after the engagement with Leefe Robinson's planes, he was able to report that the

Bristol fighter was no use to the Allies. This would prove to be a moment of overexuberance; once the British got experience with their new planes they put them to good use, and they would turn the tide of battle later in the summer.

The success of Bloody April came in part from a shift in German military tactics towards defense in depth. Reports from anti-aircraft guns created an early warning system that gave the Germans notice of Allied air attacks, and they were able to stop almost all French reconnaissance flights, severely hampering enemy intelligence and artillery operations. By now, scout planes were being used in a variety of roles, including those originally reserved for the slower planes. They fought other aircraft for domination of the skies, dropped bombs, strafed enemy troops with their guns, and provided reconnaissance of enemy formations, the last activity often being combined with the others.

The victory to which Richthofen and his men contributed led to mutinies in the French army which endangered the whole Allied war effort, and by the end of April, von Richthofen had shot down a total of 52 planes, killing 56 men and wounding or leading to the capture of 26 more. This partly came down to hard work; he would take his squadron up twice as often as many other commanders, keeping them in constant action.

The Red Baron was also responsible for a trend still in use among airforces today. Ever since his days with Boelcke, von Richthofen had flown a plane painted entirely in red, earning him his legendary nickname and at least a bit of derision among other German fliers. Von Richthofen relayed one other German pilot's anecdote: "In the Squadron to which he belonged there was a rumor that the Red Machine was occupied by a girl, by a kind of Jeanne d'Arc. He was intensely surprised when I assured him that the supposed girl was standing in front of him. He did not intend to make a joke. He was actually convinced that only a girl could sit in the extravagantly painted machine."

Undeterred, von Richthofen encouraged similarly bright schemes among the men under his command. Starting out as an improvement on colored tassels used to identify a squadron leader's plane, the decoration of planes became a phenomenon in its own right, despite the development of patterned fabrics meant to make aircraft harder to spot. Von Richthofen let the rest of the squadron paint their planes however they wanted as long as no one else used his all red scheme. Variations on their leader's colors were popular, with one pilot having a red plane with black control surfaces, while Richthofen's own brother Lothar chose a similar scheme, but with yellow instead of black.

The spectacular colors and roaming lifestyle earned the squadron the nickname of the Flying Circus, and their distinctive planes let the enemy know that they were facing Germany's deadliest pilots. Everyone in the air force wanted to associate themselves with the glamour of the Circus, and before long, other squadrons were painting their aircraft bright colors in imitation of the famed Red Baron and his men.

On August 28, 1917, Germany unveiled a new plane, the Fokker Dr.I triplane. Von Richthofen himself soon adopted the Triplane, and it became strongly associated with the mystique of the Red Baron. Highly maneuverable and with a great rate of climb, it sacrificed speed to achieve this level of agility. The Triplane proved highly effective for the Germans, who were fighting their defensive battles over their own territory, and its significant disadvantage in speed seldom became apparent. In the hands of the Flying Circus, the Triplane briefly provided a match for the newer Allied planes.

Richthofen's all-red Fokker Dr.I 425/17 shortly before his demise

The Red Baron's Fokker

Oliver Thiele's picture of a replica of Richthofen's Fokker Dr.I triplane

However, the Triplane had a significant defect, one which became apparent as fighting heated up during the Battle of Cambrai that November. Now in almost constant service, the Triplane proved vulnerable to an internal weakness: in long dives, the canvas tended to tear away from the upper wing, often leading the whole structure to collapse. Good pilots were lost not to enemy fire but to their own planes giving way beneath them, and a plane that disintegrated in a dive was useless to an air force whose tactics involved diving from above against the enemy, and who were participating in the whirling, up and down melees that by then were taking place between a hundred or more planes on each side.

It was a big enough challenge to produce thousands of aircraft, but finding the men to pilot them proved as difficult as manufacturing the machines themselves. The Germans had done better than the Allies in training their pilots, but the MAS now faced a terrible choice. On the one hand, they could pull men out of the training schools and reserves to fight on the front lines, shoring up the numbers in combat but harming training and strategic flexibility. On the other hand, they could maintain a robust infrastructure of well-trained pilots but leave the front line formations undermanned in the face of growing Allied numbers. The careful application of their own resources could only carry them so far under such circumstances.

By 1918, Germany's fortunes in the skies were falling. An Allied blockade was throttling German industry, making it impossible to maintain levels of aircraft production, and the violence had also taken its toll. In the three years leading up to September 1918, the MAS lost 2,000 planes and 11,000 men, enough to wipe out the pre-war air force several times over. These difficulties reflected the wider picture of the war, during which Germany found itself out-produced by the Allied industrial machine.

Chapter 6: Miscellaneous Weapons

Sheer ingenuity was required to develop such a vast array of means of destruction that engineers, gunsmiths, scientists and soldiers displayed in World War I, but artillery, rifles, tanks, and planes didn't account for all of it. There were a whole host of other weapons deployed during the conflict, ranging from the dreaded *flammenwerfer* (flamethrower) of the German assault troops to the canisters of poison gas fired by the artillery of virtually all the great powers, as well as a range of less conventional weapons from fragmentation grenades to handmade clubs, knives, and hatchets for trench clearing.

The close confines of trench warfare meant that troops frequently had to clear bunkers or small rooms packed with enemy soldiers ready to fire, and it rapidly became apparent that attempting to charge these miniature redoubts, even with automatic weapons, was a fast route to getting shot. Accordingly, for the first time in centuries, soldiers returned to an old weapon: the hand grenade. These had existed for centuries, and indeed, before being phased out in the 18th and 19th centuries as unreliable, they had been the principal weapons of the grenadiers, who still remained among most armies' elite formations despite having abandoned their distinctive weapon. They had seen use in naval warfare, where cramped decks and sealed rooms filled with hostile sailors (not to mention a vastly flammable environment) made them particularly effective well into the 19th century. However, there were virtually none available, or in general service, with any army at the commencement of the war. Although some initial designs were experimented with, these proved to be impractical and dangerous, and soldiers resorted to constructing their own, sometimes surprisingly complex "IEDs" out of ration tins, shell powder, scrap metal and fuses.

By 1915, however, the British had designed, tested and issued a new weapon to their troops. This was the Mills Bomb, the first modern fragmentation grenade. The Mills Bomb had the distinctive "pineapple" shape which people still associate with hand grenades, and it consisted of a packed charge which exploded the "cubes" of its casing outwards at anyone unfortunate enough to be nearby. It was operated by pulling the ring-pin out of the case, which ignited a fuse and gave the user a 7-second delay to take cover. This delay would later be shortened, as it was reckoned too long for effective use, but despite this problem it was a highly effective tool. 75 million Mills Bombs were manufactured during World War I for Allied use. In turn, the Germans developed their own design based on the same principle: the notorious *stielhandgranate* ("stick grenade" or "potato masher"). With its iconic cylinder head and long wooden handle, it was used in both World Wars.

Mills bombs

Even with grenades, clearing bunkers and trenches was still a difficult affair, especially since the long delay in the fuse meant that enemies could play "hot potato" with them by throwing them back. Accordingly, the Germans set about finding alternate ways of clearing trenches, and one of the most horrifying means of doing so was developed: the flamethrower. Although the Allies also experimented with flamethrower designs, they were not successful and saw limited use, with some being reconfigured to launch poison gas shells at short ranges. The flamethrower only entered other nation's arsenals during World War II, when it was used in Europe and the Pacific and mounted aboard tanks. It remained in service until the early 1970s, when it was unilaterally withdrawn from arsenals by most militaries due to its perceived inhumanity.

The German variant of World War I was man-portable, unlike its competitors, and followed the design most commonly associated with it: a large tank of ignitable fuel (in this case petrol) mounted on the user's back with a hose-like nozzle to spray it and a pilot light to ignite it at its head. The tank itself could be ignited by a well-placed tracer, making the user particularly vulnerable (especially as flamethrower crews were particularly hated and risked being killed out of hand if captured alive), and it had a limited range of around 20 yards, meaning that it could only be used effectively if trenches were very close together. It goes without saying that crossing no-man's-land with the cumbersome fuel tank was an extremely risky proposition, so flamethrowers had limited success as an offensive weapon, but they carried an extremely powerful psychological impact, and the Germans went on to employ them in over 300 engagements after initially trying them at Verdun in 1915.

A flamethrower during World War I

Another weapon deeply feared by all combatants during World War I was poison gas, perhaps the most notorious aspect of the war. Poison gas came in many varieties, from vescicant (blistering agent) to irritant to fully lethal, and it was usually fired by artillery. The dreaded call of *"Gas! Gas! Gas!"* was followed by a desperate scramble for masks and protective gear, in the hope that early designs, notoriously chancy, would not fail and leave the user to die a slow, agonizing death. As H. Allen put it in his book *Towards the Flame* (1934), "It was remarked as a joke that if someone yelled 'Gas', everyone in France would put on a mask. ... Gas shock was as frequent as shell shock."

A picture of British troops blinded by gas at the Battle of Estaires in 1918

A picture of British soldiers killed by a gas attack

Despite being viewed as a prohibited and unethical weapon, gas was commonly used by the Germans, French, Russians and British, with thousands of tons manufactured and used during the course of the war. Rather than used as an offensive weapon against enemy troops, it tended to be used as an area-denial weapon to prevent troops from engaging in flanking assaults or reoccupying positions they had abandoned. This was after early experiments of using it as an attack weapon led to instances of "chemical friendly fire," with troops running into positions where the gas used to drive out the defenders had still not fully dissipated. Furthermore, firing gas too close to the attacking positions could also lead to it drifting back into the gunners' trenches depending on the wind, making it a chancy weapon.

A picture of a poison gas attack during the war

However, as a psychological force and one capable of causing mass casualties among unprepared or ill-equipped troops, poison gas was unparalleled. Initial attempts at irritant gases were barely noticed, or in some cases froze due to inclement weather, but the Germans were soon able to manufacture and deploy an effective lethal agent: chlorine gas. The British responded by using phosgene gas (as did the French and Germans), but the most effective was the vescicant mustard gas, which was highly effective despite rarely being lethal. Mustard gas casualties suffered widespread blisters all over their bodies, as well as temporary (and sometimes permanent) blindness and lesions on their lungs which caused difficulty breathing. Mustard gas casualties were difficult to treat, as the gas in liquid droplet form could be transferred by contact, thus "infecting" medics.

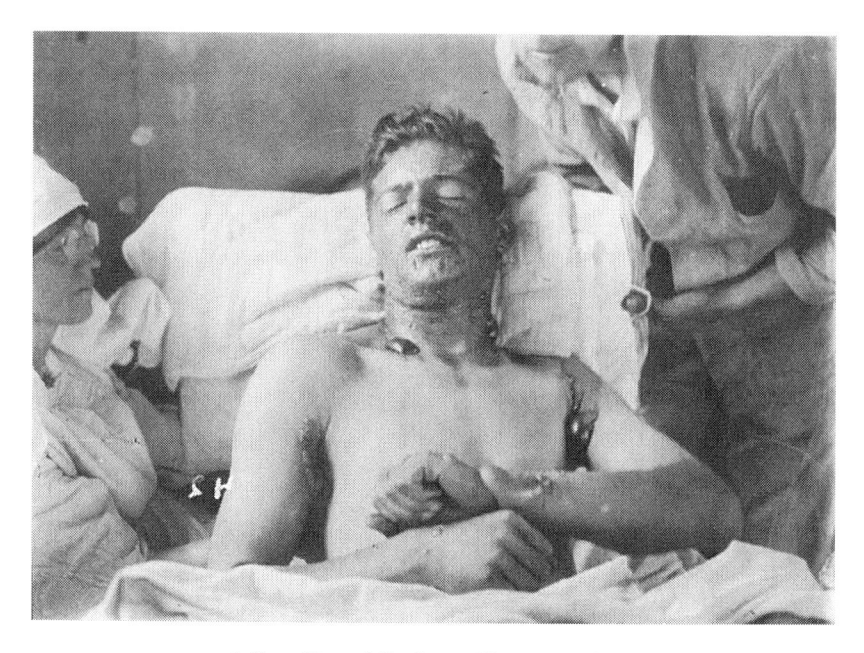

A Canadian soldier burned by mustard gas

Allied soldiers with gas masks on at Ypres

For example, in just one day at the Battle of Verdun, the Germans bombarded the French batteries with over 100,000 gas canisters of chlorine-phosgene, and though the gas had been used before and frontline troops had been issued with gas masks to combat its adverse effects, nothing could effectively prepare soldiers for the choking horror it inspired. Those unfortunate souls who were too slow to put on their masks at the dreaded cry of *"Gas! Gas! Gas!,"* along with those whose masks were damaged or defective (an all too common problem) and those who had simply lost them in the fighting choked to death as their lungs were seared by the gas and filled with fluid. All the while, their stricken comrades were unable to help or do anything other than watch the ghastly sight. 1,600 French soldiers were killed or incapacitated by the gas, which also acted as an area denial weapon. Heavier than air, the gas collected in lethal pockets at the bottom of trenches and shell-craters, meaning vast swaths of the French batteries were completely inaccessible to those artillerymen who had managed to flee the toxic shelling.

A few weeks later at Verdun, the German artillery began a comprehensive preliminary bombardment. As during the recent successful offensive, the German guns targeted the French artillery batteries with gas canisters, firing 60,000 poison shells in an attempt to kill the gunners or drive them out of their positions. However, the French had recently received a new, improved version of their standard-issue M2 gas mask. These new masks had separate eye pieces and were supplied in a variety of sizes, meaning that they were less likely to incur damage when stored and also fit their users better, thereby reducing the likelihood of leaks. Thanks to the new masks, the French artillerymen were able to stay in their positions and, despite heavy gas shelling, incurred minimal casualties while managing to continue firing their pieces.

Soldiers wearing M2 gas masks

Manufacturing poison gas shells was a vastly complex technological process, and developing the suitable agents took years of experimentation. On the opposite end of the scale – and at the sharp end of the stick – were the weapons manufactured by infantrymen to engage in hand-to-hand fighting. Although officially issued with bayonets for the task of clearing trenches (and sometimes not issued with rounds prior to the assault to ensure they did not stop to return fire and thus slow the momentum of an attack), soldiers often found that the long, sword-bladed designs were impractical because they remained stuck in the bodies of their enemies, leaving them defenseless themselves. Thus, a variety of unconventional weapons were designed.

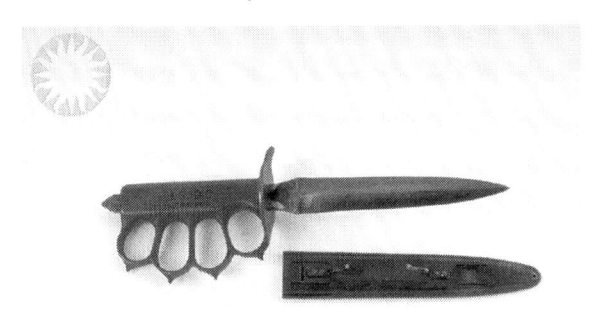

United States M1918 Trench Knife

The United States was the only army to issue an official "trench knife", a combination dagger/knuckleduster/skullbreaker, but this was based on a variety of unofficial and custom-made designs. Soldiers would file down knives or bayonets to make stilettos which could be immediately retrieved after stabbing an enemy, often with the addition of heavy knuckleduster-type guards. Likewise, punch-knives were popular designs and easy to improvise, as were filed-down "spike" bayonets. Swords, although technically issued to officers, were useless ceremonial weapons which were never carried into battle, particularly as they served to mark them out for snipers.

In addition to a variety of knives and knuckledusters, soldiers also frequently carried axes or hatchets, issued to engineer units, into battle, as well as homemade clubs manufactured by wrapping barbed wire or hammering nails into wooden handles. The small single-handed shovels which were issued ostensibly to dig in were also converted to weapons by sharpening their edge repetitively and turning them into what was effectively a hatchet.

To combat this vast array of means of destruction, body armor made its reappearance on the battlefield for the first time in awhile (except for the specially equipped heavy cavalry "cuirassier" units of the 19th century). It quickly became apparent in the opening months of World War I that the vast amounts of shrapnel produced by modern artillery required some form of protective headgear, and to defend against it, steel helmets became general issue to all troops. Each army developed their own, distinctive helmet, with the British (and Americans) opting for the iconic soup-plate design. The Germans and Austrians originally issued their famous "spiked" variant before then moving to a far more modern, sloping version which, improved upon in World War II, inspired the design of the U.S. Army Helmet in use from the 1980s until the early 2000s.

While this armor was standard-issue to all troops, a large number of inventors and salesmen (some well-meaning, others little more than conmen) produced body armor for private purchase. This came in a variety of forms, from heavy steel breastplates to coats of interlocking scale armor, and it was sometimes employed by specialist troops, such as machine gunners or soldiers on sentry duty (whose prolonged static position could prove an irresistible lure to snipers). However, very few of these body armors could protect against a rifle or machine gun bullet, and as a consequence they saw limited use. Indeed, they could frequently lead to worse injuries than might otherwise have been the case because a bullet or piece of shrapnel could drive scraps of armor into the wearer's body. Although some designs, like armored gauntlets fitted with knives for punching enemies, were more successful, body armor was not popular among troops, who sometimes considered soldiers wearing it to be cowards.

Chapter 7: Conclusion

The weapons discussed above is by no means exhaustive, but it would be nearly impossible to create a fully comprehensive list. Soldiers in World War I went so far as to use elephant guns, designed for civilian big game hunting, as weapons against enemy armor, just another testament to the variety of killing engines which were deployed during World War I. The list is endless when taking into account the variations of artillery firing everything from gas to flame to high-explosive shells, machine guns, rapid-fire rifles, semi-automatic pistols, submachineguns, zeppelins, warplanes, hand-grenades, submarines, anti-tank rifles, flamethrowers, superguns, and tanks. Although World War I also brought some valuable innovations in other fields – such as the development of stainless steel, air traffic control, and other everyday essentials such as the sanitary napkin, the zipper, and the wristwatch – as well as important breakthroughs in medicine and trauma treatment, its overwhelming contribution to progress was in the field of warfare and destruction. It was the first truly industrial war, and until World War II, most people assumed it was the peak of what Robert Burns termed "man's inhumanity to man".

A century later, it is still difficult for words to convey the horrors of warfare during World War I. Shelling was a constant feature of daily life, yet it was still impossible to grow accustomed to the random, erratic fall of bombs which could strike either randomly or with seemingly deadly efficiency. The concentrated terror of a preliminary bombardment, when individual explosions merged into one long, continuous roar, is virtually unimaginable for anyone who hasn't experienced it. In addition to that, soldiers had to worry about enemy snipers, machine gun fire, strafing runs from enemy fighter aircraft, and the dreaded poison gas which would leave men to asphyxiate slowly on the fluids from their ravaged lungs, choking like beached fish. The lottery of horrors was replete with grisly choices, and that was without factoring in the naked violence of hand-to-hand trench warfare, where rifle-butts and bayonets were practically merciful instruments of destruction compared to trench knives, knuckledusters, entrenching spades with sharpened edges, clubs wrapped with barbed wire and studded with nails, and flame throwers. For those fortunate enough to avoid becoming a casualty in one of those ways, they still had to worry about diseases, from common flu and dysentery to more deadly problems like pneumonia, tuberculosis, and gangrenous wounds.

Even with frequent rotations away from the frontline, during which the Allied troops – but not their German counterparts – were able to get some respite from the unrelenting destruction, the psychological impact of the utter devastation all around was enormous. Millions of tons of high explosives ripped apart the landscape on a scale reminiscent of a nuclear holocaust. Woods were flattened or torn apart by shellfire, and what remained of them were scavenged for firewood or to reinforce trenches. Villages and forts were reduced to piles of rubble that were scarcely recognizable as buildings. Any scrap of elevation was transformed into an artillery emplacement or, in some cases, battered down to ground level by constant shellfire. The ground itself was churned and truffled beyond all recognition, stripped completely of any blade of grass and turned into a muddy morass which clung to boots and into which soldiers sank to the knee. The landscape was pockmarked by shell-craters like the surface of the moon, and their sides were so slippery that soldiers who were unlucky enough to fall into them or dive into them for shelter from a barrage were unable to crawl out without help. In some cases, soldiers even drowned in the stagnant water that collected at the bottom of these holes. In winter, the ground froze solid and snow piled in high drifts in the trenches, adding frostbite and trenchfoot to the list of extreme miseries the soldiers were liable to suffer from.

A 2005 picture of part of the battlefield of Verdun demonstrates the destruction of artillery

Throughout the war, corpses littered the landscape, as did broken or discarded equipment. Although attempts were made to bury the dead, troops were often too exhausted to do so. If men were killed in no man's land, barring a truce to collect and bury the dead and tend to the wounded, there was no opportunity to attend to them, so they just rotted where they lay. No one would be foolish enough to risk sniper or machine gun fire to bury the dead, so they were forced to watch as bodies slowly fell apart in their uniforms, and the living had to endure the macabre stench of death. Soldiers who were killed in the opening hours of a multi-day offensive barrage were also liable to lie exposed in the trenches where they had been cut down for several days, their friends and comrades sheltering from the barrage just feet away watching them putrefy at their side. After an unsuccessful assault, the wounded who had the misfortune not to be rescued might scream in agony for days, shredding their comrades' nerves.

Put simply, World War I was combat at its most brutal and horrific, and it is easy to see why it continues to leave a lasting impact on Europe's collective memory.

Bibliography

Readers interested in learning more about the weapons employed in World War I should consult Chris Bishop's *The Illustrated Encyclopaedia of Weapons of World War I* or Ian Westwell's *The Illustrated History of the Weapons of World War I*. For more specific texts, see David Fletcher's *Great War Tank Manual* or Dale Clarke's *World War I Battlefield Artillery Tactics*. For a harrowing, semi-fictionalised account of how wielding and being on the receiving end of these weapons, see Erich Maria Remarque's classic novel, *All Quiet on the Western Front*.

Other Sources

Bull, S. (2003). Trench warfare. PRC Publishing. ISBN 1-85648-657-5.

Edmonds, James Edward; Wynne, Graeme Chamley (1927). Military Operations: France and Belgium, 1915, volume 1. Macmillan and co., limited.

Haber, L. F. (1986). The Poisonous Cloud; Chemical Warfare in the First World War. Oxford University Press. ISBN 0-19-858142-4.

Harris, R.; Paxman, J. (2002). A Higher Form of Killing : The Secret History of Chemical and Biological Warfare. Random House Trade Paperbacks. ISBN 0-8129-6653-8. (first published 1982)

Jones, Simon (2007). World War I Gas Warfare Tactics and Equipment. Osprey. ISBN 978-1-84603-151-9.

Palazzo, Albert (2000). Seeking Victory on the Western Front: The British Army & Chemical Warfare in World War 1. U of Nebraska press. ISBN 0-8032-8774-7.

Winter, D. (1978). Death's Men: Soldiers of the Great War. Penguin Books. ISBN 0-14-016822-2.

Cheesman, E.F. (ed.) Fighter Aircraft of the 1914–1918 War. Letchworth, UK: Harleyford, 1960

Gray, Peter & Thetford, Owen German Aircraft of the First World War. London, Putnam, 1962.

Herris, Jack & Pearson, Bob Aircraft of World War I. London, Amber Books, 2010. ISBN 978-1-906626-65-5.

Morrow, John. German Air Power in World War I. Lincoln: University of Nebraska Press, 1982. Contains design and production figures, as well as economic influences.

Pearson, George, Aces: A Story of the First Air War, historical advice by Brereton Greenhous and Philip Markham, NFB, 1993. Contains assertion aircraft created trench stalemate.

Terraine, John White Heat: the new warfare 1914-18. London, Guild Publishing, 1982

Printed in Great Britain
by Amazon